RELAXING SERENITY
COLORING BOOK FOR ADULTS & TEENS

Therapeutic Art Therapy Coloring
for Relaxation, Stress Relief, Anxiety Relief

Sale of this book without a front cover may be unauthorized. If this book is without a cover, it may have been reported to the publisher as "unsold and/or destroyed" and neither the author nor publisher may have received payment for it.

This coloring book offers a creative outlet; engaging in coloring activities can be a positive and enjoyable experience. However, it is not a substitute for professional medical advice, diagnosis, or treatment. If you have specific mental health concerns, please consult a qualified healthcare professional. The author, designer, and publisher disclaim any liability for any consequences resulting from the use of this coloring book. Use it at your discretion, and if you disagree with these terms, kindly refrain from using this book for therapeutic purposes.

The patterns within the illustrations contained in this book are products of imagination. Any resemblance to existing coloring books or coloring pages is entirely coincidental and unintentional.

Relaxing Serenity Coloring Book For Adults & Teens

Copyright © 2023 by Jule Tori
All rights reserved.
No part of this publication may be reproduced or transmitted in any form or by any means, electronic or mechanical, including photocopying, recording, or by any information storage and retrieval system, without prior express written consent from the copyright owner, except for the inclusion of brief quotations and/or illustration examples in a product review.

Designed and published by Jule Tori

ISBN: 978-1-7382157-1-3 (hardcover)
ISBN: 978-1-7382157-0-6 (paperback)

Relaxing Serenity

This relaxing coloring book is designed to help you unwind, de-stress, and discover the therapeutic power of creativity. Transform with the healing power of art therapy as you bring your chosen designs to life. Get ready to embark on a soothing journey through a symphony of colors and patterns. Start your voyage to relaxation, stress relief, and anxiety relief!

∞

The illustrations are printed on one side only to minimize color bleed-through.

To protect upcoming pages, we recommend placing additional blank pieces of paper under the page you're working on, as needed. Or you can cut out individual pages for coloring.

Use the test color page provided to test your coloring media to see how it will look first before beginning your art project.

Relaxing Serenity

Test Color Page

Relaxing Serenity

Relaxing Serenity

Relaxing Serenity

Relaxing Serenity

Relaxing Serenity

Relaxing Serenity

Relaxing Serenity

Relaxing Serenity

Relaxing Serenity

Relaxing Serenity

Relaxing Serenity

Relaxing Serenity

Relaxing Serenity

Relaxing Serenity

Relaxing Serenity

Relaxing Serenity

Relaxing Serenity

Relaxing Serenity

Relaxing Serenity

Relaxing Serenity

Relaxing Serenity

Relaxing Serenity

Relaxing Serenity

Relaxing Serenity

Relaxing Serenity

Relaxing Serenity

Relaxing Serenity

Relaxing Serenity

Relaxing Serenity

Relaxing Serenity

Relaxing Serenity

Relaxing Serenity

Relaxing Serenity

Relaxing Serenity

Relaxing Serenity

Relaxing Serenity

Relaxing Serenity

Relaxing Serenity

Relaxing Serenity

Relaxing Serenity

Relaxing Serenity

Relaxing Serenity

Relaxing Serenity

www.ingramcontent.com/pod-product-compliance
Lightning Source LLC
Chambersburg PA
CBHW050806220426
43209CB00088BA/1654